101 Wordy Phrases

A Vocabula 101 Series Handbook

101 Wordy Phrases

Robert Hartwell Fiske

Vocabula Books
Rockport, Massachusetts

These 101 entries are based on the content of *The Dictionary of Concise Writing* (Marion Street Press).

101 Wordy Phrases. Copyright © 2005 Vocabula Communications Company. All rights reserved. No part of this book may be reproduced in any form or by any electronic or mechanical means including information storage and retrieval systems without permission in writing from the publisher, except by a reviewer who may quote brief passages in a review. Published by Vocabula Books, an imprint of Vocabula Communications Company, 5A Holbrook Court, Rockport, Massachusetts 01966. (978) 546-3911. First edition.

VOCABULA is a registered service mark of Vocabula Communications Company. THE VOCABULA REVIEW is a registered service mark of Vocabula Communications Company. GRUMBLING ABOUT GRAMMAR is a registered service mark of Vocabula Communications Company. A SOCIETY IS GENERALLY AS LAX AS ITS LANGUAGE and WELL SPOKEN IS HALF SUNG are registered service marks of Vocabula Communications Company. *The Vocabula Review* logo is a registered trademark of Vocabula Communications Company. All six marks are registered in the U.S. Patent and Trademark Office.

Library of Congress Control Number: 2005936110

Cover design and page layout by Ruth Maassen

Read *The Vocabula Review* at www.vocabula.com.

Vocabula Books
an imprint of
Vocabula Communications Company

*Presented to*_____

*By*_____

*Date*_____

To Brad

Vocabula 101 Series Handbooks

101 Wordy Phrases
101 Foolish Phrases
101 Elegant Paragraphs
101 Scarcely Used Words (forthcoming)

Other Books by Robert Hartwell Fiske

The Dictionary of Disagreeable English, Deluxe Edition (Writer's Digest Books, 2006)

The Dictionary of Concise Writing (Marion Street Press, second edition, 2006)

The Dimwit's Dictionary (Marion Street Press, second edition, 2006)

Vocabula Bound: Outbursts, Insights, Explanations, and Oddities (editor) (Marion Street Press, 2004)

About the Author

Robert Hartwell Fiske is the editor and publisher of *The Vocabula Review* (www.vocabula.com), a monthly online journal about the English language, and *Vocabula Bound Quarterly*, a quarterly print publication.

Introduction

Inadequate though they may be, words distinguish us from all other living things. Only we humans can reflect on the past and plan for the future; it is language that allows us to do so. Indeed, our worth is partly in our words. Effective use of language — clear writing and speaking — is a measure of our humanness.

When they do their work best, words help people communicate; they promote understanding between people. And this, being well understood, is precisely the goal we should all aspire to when writing and speaking. As obvious as this seems, it is not a goal we commonly achieve.

Words often ill serve their purpose. When they do their work badly, words militate against us. Poor grammar, sloppy syntax, abused words, misspelled words, and other infelicities of style impede communication and advance only misunderstanding.

But there is another, perhaps less well-known, obstacle to effective communication: too many words.

We often believe that many words are better than few. Perhaps we imagine that the more we say, the more we know or the more others will think we know, or that the more obscure our writing is, the more profound our thoughts are. Seldom, of course, is this so. Wordiness is arguably the biggest obstacle to clear writing and speaking. But it is also more than that.

• *Wordiness is an obstacle to success.* Almost all professional people know that success in business partly depends on good communications skills, on writing and speaking clearly and persuasively. Businesspeople who cannot express themselves well are often at a disadvantage in the corporate world.

• *Wordiness is an obstacle to companionship.* Few of us enjoy being with someone who speaks incessantly or incoherently. Wordiness in others may make us impatient; it may annoy us, and we may think it rude. Worse than that, when we have difficulty understanding someone, sooner or later we may not care what it is that he tries to convey. We lose interest in what a person says and, ultimately, in who a person is.

• *Wordiness is an obstacle to self-knowledge.* A superfluity of words conceals more than it reveals. We need time to be silent and still, time to reflect on the past and think about the future; without it, no one is knowable.

Wordiness is an obstacle to these goals and others. Whatever your profession, whatever your personality, wordiness is a condition for which we all should seek a cure.

1. a bigger (greater; higher; larger) degree (extent) (of) *more*.

• Whereas the UC-Davis site assumed users want to focus on extensive reading, the American Girls site assumed users want *a higher degree of* graphics, less external linking, and briefer and simpler sections of text. Whereas the UC-Davis site assumed users want to focus on extensive reading, the American Girls site assumed users want *more* graphics, less external linking, and briefer and simpler sections of text. • Politicians and public officials should be required to tolerate *a greater degree of* criticism than ordinary citizens. Politicians and public officials should be required to tolerate *more* criticism than ordinary citizens. • One can speculate whether concentrating all the army special forces units in one regiment is the most appropriate solution or if *a bigger degree of* diversification would contribute to achieving more specialization and introduce a competitive factor among the units. One can speculate whether concentrating all the army special forces units in one regiment is the most appropriate solution or if *more* diversification would contribute to achieving more specialization and introduce a competitive factor among the units. • *A bigger extent of* improvement was prevented by the HUF 197 million of cash contribution made by BC Rt. to promote the development of its subsidiaries. *More* improvement was prevented by the HUF 197 million of cash contribution made by BC Rt. to promote the development of its subsidiaries.

2. (a; the)...action delete.

• Thai police increased patrols at international schools in Bangkok and around popular tourist resorts after receiving intelligence information about potential *terrorist action*. Thai police increased patrols at international schools in Bangkok and around popular tourist resorts after receiving intelligence information about potential *terrorism*. • Jailing Danilov was *retaliatory action* against the seizure of a Soviet agent in the United States. Jailing Danilov was *retaliation* against the seizure of a Soviet agent in the United States. • We are taking steps to revoke the security clearances of individuals who have been involved in *illegal actions*. We are taking steps to revoke the security clearances of individuals who have been involved in *illegalities*. • The *innovative actions* of the European Regional Development Fund are laboratories of ideas for disadvantaged regions. The *innovations* of the European Regional Development Fund are laboratories of ideas for disadvantaged regions.

3. a (the) decreased (decreasing) number of *fewer.*

• The financial position of the healthcare system has become more and more strained, and this in turn has resulted in *a decreased number of* hospital beds. The financial position of the healthcare system has become more and more strained, and this in turn has resulted in *fewer* hospital beds. • This means there are *a decreased number of* pellets being shot at the target. This means there are *fewer* pellets being shot at the target. • In particular, it has led to a dramatic decline in the profitability of Japanese small businesses and *decreasing numbers of* small firms. In particular, it has led to a dramatic decline in the profitability of Japanese small businesses and *fewer* small firms.

4. a lesser (lower; smaller) degree (extent) (of) *less.*

• Transparent WDM systems offer *a lesser degree of* monitoring and network capability than TDM systems. Transparent WDM systems offer *less* monitoring and network capability than TDM systems. • The less common plants are given *a smaller degree of* treatment not just because of their limited use in food production but because of their scarcity on sites. The less common plants are given *less* treatment not just because of their limited use in food production but because of their scarcity on sites. • Most land areas in China have *a lower extent of* soil degradation. Most land areas in China have *less* soil degradation.

5. (what is) a (the) manner (means; mechanism; method; procedure; process; technique) by which *how.*

• *The manner by which* the man ultimately inflicts himself on his companion is, of course, immaterial. *How* the man ultimately inflicts himself on his companion is, of course, immaterial. • We will now examine *the process by which* natural and global marketing activities are controlled. We will now examine *how* natural and global marketing activities are controlled. • *What is the means by which* a nation can increase investment? *How* can a nation increase investment? • The answer should describe *a process by which* all corners are equally likely to be chosen. The answer should describe *how* all corners are equally likely to be chosen.

6. **(a; the)...amount of time (length of time; period of time; span of time)** *period; time; while;* delete.

• They filmed our arguments over *a three-month period of time.* They filmed our arguments over *three months.* • You can get to know someone very well if you date him or her for a long enough *period of time.* You can get to know someone very well if you date him or her for a long enough *while.* • But over the same *length of time,* inflation averaged 3 percent a year. But over the same *period*, inflation averaged 3 percent a year.

7. **(a; the) -ance (-ence) of** *-ing.*

• With such asset and liability opportunities, *the avoidance of* large credit losses was a practical management consideration in ensuring attractive profitability. With such asset and liability opportunities, *avoiding* large credit losses was a practical management consideration in ensuring attractive profitability. • In *the performance of* their routines, they are acting as extensions of your position. In *performing* their routines, they are acting as extensions of your position. • A recent variation on providing ver-

as the basis for (-ing) 5

sion protection has been liquidation of the product on site by *issuance of* a credit to the retailer. A recent variation on providing version protection has been liquidation of the product on site by *issuing* a credit to the retailer.

8. as the basis for (-ing) *for (-ing); so as to; to.*

• Data is any information used *as the basis for discussing or deciding* something. Data is any information used *to discuss or decide* something. • The purpose of the course is to provide an understanding of physics *as a basis for successfully launching* new high-tech ventures. The purpose of the course is to provide an understanding of physics *so as to successfully launch* new high-tech ventures. • We can use their modern ecological requirements *as a basis for interpreting* what past environments must have been like. We can use their modern ecological requirements *to interpret* what past environments must have been like.

9. based on the fact that *because; considering; for; given; in that; since.*

• I'm not in favor of it *based on the fact that* a lot of small businesses will suffer. I'm not in favor of it *because* a lot of small businesses will suffer. • *Based on the fact that* no single timing rule works well all the time, AIQ incorporates many rules that work together in a powerful synergism to signal when the overall market, and individual securities, are ready to move. *Since* no single timing rule works well all the time, AIQ incorporates many rules that work together in a powerful synergism to signal when the overall market, and individual securities, are ready to move.

10. **(please) be advised (informed) that** delete.

• *Please be advised that* we must be notified at least two weeks prior to your closing date in order to issue your 6(d) certificate. We must be notified at least two weeks prior to your closing date in order to issue your 6(d) certificate. • However, *please be advised that* this person is out of town until next week; I am sure she will then respond to you at her earliest possible convenience. However, this person is out of town until next week; I am sure she will then respond to you at her earliest possible convenience.

11. **because of the fact that** *because; considering; for; given; in that; since.*

• *Because of the fact that* they are still monopoly suppliers of local exchange, I also see a discouraging prospect for the operating companies in this area. *Since* they are still monopoly suppliers of local exchange, I also see a discouraging prospect for the operating companies in this area. • I discounted these things *because of the fact that* I cared so much for you. I discounted these things *because* I cared so much for you. • We know there is a game *because of the fact that* there are a lot of people waiting in line. We know there is a game *because* there are a lot of people waiting in line.

12. **come into (to) (a; the)...(of)** delete.

• Eventually they *came to the recognition* that the supercomputer business is a high stakes poker game. Eventually they *recognized* that the supercomputer business is a high stakes poker game. •

It neither glosses over the true historical picture nor attempts to *come to the defense of* any individuals. It neither glosses over the true historical picture nor attempts to *defend* any individuals. • We must *come to the understanding* that we are on a journey, and in that journey, it is not so much where we are at present but where we are going. We must *understand* that we are on a journey, and in that journey, it is not so much where we are at present but where we are going.

13. comparatively -(i)er than (less than; more than) *-(i)er than (less than; more than).*

• U.S. experts say the Soviet budget deficit that Moscow has finally acknowledged is *comparatively larger than* that of America. U.S. experts say the Soviet budget deficit that Moscow has finally acknowledged is *larger than* that of America. • *Comparatively,* Benin is slightly *smaller than* the state of Pennsylvania. Benin is slightly *smaller than* the state of Pennsylvania.

14. compared (contrasted) to (with)...relatively *compared (contrasted) to (with); -(i)er than (less than; more than).*

• *Compared to* the advantages, there are *relatively* few disadvantages for a sole proprietorship. *Compared to* the advantages, there are few disadvantages for a sole proprietorship. • The primary effect appears to be a loss of plutonium from a diseased liver with possible redistribution to the skeleton when *compared to relatively* healthy individuals. The primary effect appears to be a loss of plutonium from a diseased liver with possible redistribution to the skeleton when *compared to* healthy individuals.

15. continue on *continue*.

• If he doesn't raise enough money, he won't be able to *continue on*. If he doesn't raise enough money, he won't be able to *continue*. • Her business is going to *continue on*. Her business is going to *continue*. • The series is set to begin at 7 pm Friday, March 26, and *continue on* Saturday, March 27, at 7 pm. The series is set to begin at 7 pm Friday, March 26, and *continue* Saturday, March 27, at 7 pm. • I hope that commitment will *continue on* indefinitely. I hope that commitment will *continue* indefinitely.

16. (a; the) critical ... in (of; to) *critical to*.

• *A critical ingredient in* a manager's philosophy of change is how much emphasis is placed on trust in the work environment. *Critical to* a manager's philosophy of change is how much emphasis is placed on trust in the work environment. • Active cooperation between all industry groups is *a critical factor* to the success of EFT and POS. Active cooperation between all industry groups is *critical* to the success of EFT and POS. • The entire landscape of faculty will change, and *a critical part of* our strategy is bringing new faces to U of T. The entire landscape of faculty will change, and *critical to* our strategy is bringing new faces to U of T.

17. (a; the)...degree of delete.

• He provides a healthy and thoughtful *degree of* skepticism about prospects for positive change at the national level. He provides a healthy and thoughtful skepticism about prospects for positive change at the national level. • Competitor reaction cannot be predicted with any *degree of* accuracy. Competitor reaction cannot be predicted with any accuracy. • This is sophisticated, suicidal and there's a *degree of* ruthlessness that we haven't ever seen in the use of terrorism before. This is sophisticated, suicidal and there's a ruthlessness that we haven't ever seen in the use of terrorism before.

18. derive pleasure from *admire; appreciate; delight in; enjoy; rejoice in; relish; savor.*

• We *derived great pleasure from* their performance. We *delighted in* their performance. • You *derive pleasure from* traditional climbing, we *derive pleasure from* making sure you'll be well outfitted with the protection you need. You *enjoy* traditional climbing, we *enjoy* making sure you'll be well outfitted with the protection you need. • Most people in the industry *derive pleasure from* working with their horses, whether it's for a hobby or profit. Most people in the industry *relish* working with their horses, whether it's for a hobby or profit.

19. despite the fact that *although; but; even though; still; though; yet.*

• *Despite the fact that* all the charts are on paper rather than on-line, the bank reports that departments competed to improve their performance. *Although* all the charts are on paper rather than on-line, the bank reports that departments competed to improve their performance. • *Despite the fact that* often they're the only green spot in a concrete and asphalt jungle, golf courses are still targeted as threats to the environment. *Though* often they're the only green spot in a concrete and asphalt jungle, golf courses are still targeted as threats to the environment. • Schumer wants to break the law *despite the fact that* Bush administration officials say the current stockpile of Cipro is adequate. Schumer wants to break the law *even though* Bush administration officials say the current stockpile of Cipro is adequate.

20. do (a; the)... (about; in; of; on; to) -*(al)ly;* delete.

• We *did a thorough search of* the area and found nothing. We *thoroughly searched* the area and found nothing. • They'd rather build a roadway than provide a program that prevents someone from *doing harm to* someone else. They'd rather build a roadway than provide a program that prevents someone from *harming* someone else. • Are we supposed to be *doing the underlining of* the title twice? Are we supposed to be *underlining* the title twice?

21. **during the course (length) of** *during; for; in; over; throughout; when; while; with.*

• *During the course of* the analysis, we suppose the array or list contains n elements. *Throughout* the analysis, we suppose the array or list contains n elements. • *During the course of* trying to negotiate with the gunmen, her husband was shot and killed. *While* trying to negotiate with the gunmen, her husband was shot and killed. • In addition, all regional students must attend one colloquium *during the length of* their enrollment. In addition, all regional students must attend one colloquium *during* their enrollment. • I wish to have my sheets replaced on a daily basis *during the length of* my stay. I wish to have my sheets replaced on a daily basis *during* my stay.

22. (a; the)... element (in; of; to) *some;* delete.

• There will always be *an element of* doubt. There will always be *some* doubt. • The florid phrases and poor editing suggest some *element of* haste in the booklet's concoction. The florid phrases and poor editing suggest some haste in the booklet's concoction. • *A* common *element* to any system is the need for continuous top-management involvement. Common to any system is the need for continuous top-management involvement.

23. engage in... (a; the) delete.

• I appreciate the straightforward way in which you've *engaged in this discussion*. I appreciate the straightforward way in which you've *discussed this*. • Known as an active force in the labor movement, the unions at the Gillette France plant are *engaged in a nationwide campaign* to shape public opinion. Known as an active force in the labor movement, the unions at the Gillette France plant are *campaigning nationwide* to shape public opinion.

24. express... (about; for; of; to) delete.

• He *expressed doubt* whether the issue would be much of a headache on the campaign trail this fall. He *doubted* whether the issue would be much of a headache on the campaign trail this fall. • Many *express open admiration for* women who are healthy, well-groomed, and confident. Many *openly admire* women who are healthy, well-groomed, and confident. • Most top executives seem to believe strongly in the need for better human relations, but they often *express distrust of* the training program itself. Most top executives seem to believe strongly in the need for better human relations, but they often *distrust* the training program itself. • We wish to *express our sincere thanks to* our special representative for her responsiveness. We wish to *sincerely thank* our special representative for her responsiveness.

25. (a; the)... factor (in; of; to) delete.

• The fact that we could not have children *was a contributing factor* to our divorce. The fact that we could not have children *contributed* to our divorce. • Knowing the consequences of obesity should be a *motivating factor* in losing weight. Knowing the consequences of obesity should be a *motivation* in losing weight. • Researchers indicate, however, that after age 50 lifestyle becomes *a less influential factor* in physiological change than aging itself. Researchers indicate, however, that after age 50 lifestyle becomes *less influential* in physiological change than aging itself.

26. first... before *before*.

• You cannot print a document on the disk that has been fast-saved unless you *first* positioned the cursor at the end of the document *before* you saved it. You cannot print a document on the disk that has been fast-saved unless you positioned the cursor at the end of the document *before* you saved it. • The only way to prevent such occurrences is to ensure that the nodes performing the restoration *first* determine the type of failure *before* invoking their restoration mechanisms. The only way to prevent such occurrences is to ensure that the nodes performing the restoration determine the type of failure *before* invoking their restoration mechanisms. • Complications due to sampling and disease need to be *first* eliminated *before* firm conclusions can be made. Complications due to sampling and disease need to be eliminated *before* firm conclusions can be made.

27. for fear (that; of)... can (could; may; might; shall; should; will; would) *lest*.

• Few of us know what to say to friends who are mourning, so we may avoid them *for fear we'll* say the wrong thing. Few of us know what to say to friends who are mourning, so we may avoid them *lest we* say the wrong thing. • The Arab League has meanwhile refused to transfer millions of dollars in aid to the PA *for fear that* top officials would lay their hands on the money. The Arab League has meanwhile refused to transfer millions of dollars in aid to the PA *lest* top officials lay their hands on the money.

28. for the purpose of (-ing) *for (-ing); so as to; to.*

• All deposited items are received *for the purpose of collection,* and all credits for deposited items are provisional. All deposited items are received *for collection,* and all credits for deposited items are provisional. • The mission of the Deaf Dog Education Action Fund is to provide education and funding *for the purpose of improving and/or saving* the lives of deaf dogs. The mission of the Deaf Dog Education Action Fund is to provide education and funding *so as to improve and/or save* the lives of deaf dogs. • Trade Council of Iceland was established in 1986 *for the purpose of promoting exports and increasing* marketing awareness among Icelandic companies. Trade Council of Iceland was established in 1986 *to promote exports and increase* marketing awareness among Icelandic companies.

29. for the (simple) reason that *because; considering; for; given; in that; since.*

• Normally, short-term Treasuries yield less than longer-term Treasuries, *for the simple reason that* investors demand to be rewarded for tying up their money in longer-term instruments. Normally, short-term Treasuries yield less than longer-term Treasuries *because* investors demand to be rewarded for tying up their money in longer-term instruments. • It's not a bestseller *for the simple reason that* people aren't brave enough to read it. It's not a bestseller *because* people aren't brave enough to read it. • However, it's essential to life *for the simple reason that* our food is one of our primary sources of qi (c'hi, or ki) after birth. However, it's essential to life *since* our food is one of our primary sources of qi (c'hi, or ki) after birth.

30. give (a; the)... (for; of; to) delete.

• *Give an estimate on* the amount of time it will take and the number of people you will need. *Estimate* the amount of time it will take and the number of people you will need. • The Book of Leviticus *gives a list of* the women who are not available to marry certain men. The Book of Leviticus *lists* the women who are not available to marry certain men. • The main purpose of choosing an outside auditor is to guarantee to insiders and interested outsiders that the financial data presented in financial documents *give an accurate representation of* events. The main purpose of choosing an outside auditor is to guarantee to insiders and interested outsiders that the financial data presented in financial documents *accurately represent* events. • They work hard; they deserve to be *given compensation*. They work hard; they deserve to be *compensated*. • Did he *give any indication of* what he plans to do? Did he *indicate* what he plans to do? • I'll *give you a call* at the end of the week. I'll *call* you at the end of the week. • I hope you will *give me consideration* for diverse projects. I hope you will *consider me* for diverse projects. • Many small businesses and private individuals are *giving serious consideration to* their energy and resource needs for the year ahead. Many small businesses and private individuals are *seriously considering* their energy and resource needs for the year ahead. • Thanks to Craig for taking the time out of his busy schedule to *give this book a* read. Thanks to Craig for taking the time out of his busy schedule to *read* this book.

31. has (a; the) ... (about; for; of; on; over) delete.

• If you *have intentions of going*, you should make your reservations now. If you *intend to go*, you should make your reservations now. • He *has control over* the entire program. He *controls* the entire program. • Boston *has the need for* a new harbor tunnel. Boston *needs* a new harbor tunnel. • The strategic partnering lawyer must *have a firm grasp of* the fundamentals of the legal principles in Europe and in the Far East. The strategic partnering lawyer must *firmly grasp* the fundamentals of the legal principles in Europe and in the Far East.

32. has (a) ... effect on (upon) *acts on; affects; bears on; influences;* delete.

• Over the past twenty years, the U.S. economy has *had a significant effect on* the Amish way of life. Over the past twenty years, the U.S. economy has *significantly influenced* the Amish way of life. • Human activity is changing the composition of the atmosphere in ways that could *have profound effects upon* life on the Earth. Human activity is changing the composition of the atmosphere in ways that could *profoundly affect* life on the Earth.

33. has occasion to be *is.*

• The ombudsman often *has occasion to be* aware of problems arising between levels and units. The ombudsman often *is* aware of problems arising between levels and units. • If he *has occasion to be* in Washington, the president likes to spend time with him. If he *is* in Washington, the president likes to spend time with him. • Some fifty years later I *had occasion to be* in the vicinity of that church and I went in, just to see. Some fifty years later I *was* in the vicinity of that church and I went in, just to see. • If you have ever *had occasion to be* deprived of your normal sleep, you know how hard it is to function when you haven't had enough rest. If you have ever *been* deprived of your normal sleep, you know how hard it is to function when you haven't had enough rest.

34. (a; the) high degree (of) *abundant; a good (great) deal (of); a good (great) many (of); ample; broad; enormous; extensive; great; high; huge; large; many (of); marked; most (of); much (of); salient; signal; significant; sizable; striking; substantial; vast;* delete.

• Tuesday's federal budget placed *a high degree of* importance on improving learning in Canada. Tuesday's federal budget placed *much* importance on improving learning in Canada. • Drug development involves *a high degree of* risk. Drug development involves *significant* risk. • One of the distinguishing characteristics of the Eurobond market is its *high degree of* competitiveness. One of the distinguishing characteristics of the Eurobond market is its *marked* competitiveness. • In 2004 U.S. exports to Canada are likely to increase on the strength of the *high degree of* integration that exists between the Canadian and U.S. pork markets. In 2004 U.S. exports to Canada are likely to increase on the strength of the *broad* integration that exists between the Canadian and U.S. pork markets.

35. (an; the) important... for (in; of; to) *important for (to)*.

• Because decision making is *an important element of* a manager's job, we need to discover anything that can improve the quality of decision making. Because decision making is *important to* a manager's job, we need to discover anything that can improve the quality of decision making. • Their willingness to commit capital was *an important factor for* success. Their willingness to commit capital was *important for* success. • Certainly, overall physical health is *an important component in* any society. Certainly, overall physical health is *important to* any society.

36. in a (the) fashion (manner; way) (in which; that) *as; like*.

• But such a scientific inquiry already took place years ago, *in the manner* provided for by law. But such a scientific inquiry already took place years ago, *as* provided for by law. • Science fiction and mystery are often mixed, but not *in the fashion that* Roberts has managed. Science fiction and mystery are often mixed, but not *as* Roberts has managed. • Zeus allows you to work intuitively *in the way that* you think best. Zeus allows you to work intuitively *as* you think best.

37. in a manner of speaking *as it were; in a sense; in a way; so to speak*; delete.

• Meanwhile by going inside the body you would be penetrating it; *in a manner of speaking*, you would have sex with it. Meanwhile by going inside the body you would be penetrating it; *in a sense*, you would have sex with it. • This time around, the company has, *in a manner of speaking*, thrown caution out of the window. This time around, the company has, *as it were*, thrown caution out of the window. • Last night, *in a manner of speaking*, he began life anew. Last night, he began life anew.

38. **in a (the)... sense** *-(al)ly;* delete.

• *In a broad sense,* office automation is the incorporation of technology to help people manage information. *Broadly,* office automation is the incorporation of technology to help people manage information. • Although there is a significant relationship *in a statistical sense,* the association is not strong. Although there is a significant *statistical* relationship, the association is not strong. • I don't mean this *in a pejorative sense.* I don't mean this *pejoratively.* • There was really nothing which could be called communication *in any genuine sense.* There was really nothing which could be called *genuine* communication.

39. **in comparison (in contrast) to (with)... relatively**
compared (contrasted) to (with); in comparison (in contrast) to (with); relatively.

• *In comparison to* earlier years, inflation has been *relatively* moderate over the last half decade. *Compared to* earlier years, inflation has been moderate over the last half decade. • America may never be a perfectly safe place to be, but it is *in comparison, relatively* the safest as well as the freest. America may never be a perfectly safe place to be, but it is *in comparison* the safest as well as the freest. • *In comparison, relatively* little is known about how developing RGCs acquire these characteristics. *Relatively* little is known about how developing RGCs acquire these characteristics. • *In contrast, relatively* little is known about the gender-specific changes in body composition that characterize AIDS wasting in women. *In contrast,* little is known about the gender-specific changes in body composition that characterize AIDS wasting in women.

40. (a; the) -ing of -*ing.*

• *The taking of drugs* is bad for people. *Taking drugs* is bad for people. • Often the initial development of a program focuses on *the obtaining of* some correct solution to the given problem. Often the initial development of a program focuses on *obtaining* some correct solution to the given problem. • It has several verification problems that can only be appreciated by *a careful reading of* the treaty. It has several verification problems that can only be appreciated by *carefully reading* the treaty.

41. in (a; the)...manner -*(al)ly;* delete.

• I hope future stories dealing with sensitive issues such as this will be handled *in a more responsible and accurate manner.* I hope future stories dealing with sensitive issues such as this will be handled *more responsibly and accurately.* • According to CAREI, studies have found that some families were *affected in a positive manner* by the start changes and some were negatively affected. According to CAREI, studies have found that some families were *positively affected* by the start changes and some were negatively affected. • All writing on labels must be printed *in a clear and legible manner* and should be in Spanish unless authorized otherwise by the DFC. All writing on labels must be printed *clearly and legibly* and should be in Spanish unless authorized otherwise by the DFC.

42. in so far as... (goes; is concerned) *about; as for; as to; concerning; for; in; of; on; over; regarding; respecting; to; toward; with;* delete.

• The president's position, *insofar as negotiations are concerned,* has never changed. The president's position *on negotiations* has never changed. • Intent, an element of the offense, may also be a factor *insofar as a vehicle's recovery and condition are concerned.* Intent, an element of the offense, may also be a factor *in a vehicle's recovery and condition.* • The ruling clarifies that the orthotics benefit in section 1861(s)(9) of the Act, *insofar as braces are concerned,* is limited to leg, arm, back, and neck braces that are used independently rather than in conjunction with, or as components of, other medical or non-medical equipment. The ruling clarifies that the orthotics benefit in section 1861(s)(9) of the Act, *regarding braces,* is limited to leg, arm, back, and neck braces that are used independently rather than in conjunction with, or as components of, other medical or non-medical equipment.

43. (condemn) in the strongest possible terms *strongly (condemn).*

• Federal drug regulators should warn physicians and patients *in the strongest possible terms* that antidepressants not only cause some children and teenagers to become suicidal but most have also failed to cure their depression. Federal drug regulators should *strongly* warn physicians and patients in the strongest possible terms that antidepressants not only cause some children and teenagers to become suicidal but most have also failed to cure their depression. • Vladimir Putin condemned *in the strongest possible terms* this barbaric act of killing the innocent and the young. Vladimir Putin *strongly* condemned this barbaric act of killing the innocent and the young. • UNRWA will protest this violation of the sanctity of its school *in the strongest possible terms* to the Israeli authorities. UNRWA will *strongly* protest this violation of the sanctity of its school to the Israeli authorities.

44. in the way (of) delete.

• This step requires that you research jobs to determine what they call for *in the way of* education, skills, and aptitudes. This step requires that you research jobs to determine what education, skills, and aptitudes they call for. • There is little motivation for long periods of foolishness, and there is much *in the way of* market discipline to prevent it. There is little motivation for long periods of foolishness, and there is much market discipline to prevent it. • A sentence such as "It is 93 million miles to the sun" does not generate much *in the way of* questions; it is too specific. A sentence such as "It is 93 million miles to the sun" does not generate many questions; it is too specific. • As parents, we got little *in the way of* help, a good deal *in the way* of confusion, and an infinite amount *in the way* of worry. As parents, we got little help, a good deal of confusion, and an infinite amount of worry.

45. irrespective of (the fact) whether... (or) *despite whether; no matter whether; regardless of whether; whether... or (not).*

• One delegate said his parish would continue to raise money for its diocese *irrespective of whether* the archdiocesan assessment is met. One delegate said his parish would continue to raise money for its diocese *whether or not* the archdiocesan assessment is met. • You need to procure the visas for all the countries, even the ones that the trains are passing through, *irrespective of the fact whether* the trains are stopping in those countries. You need to procure the visas for all the countries, even the ones that the trains are passing through, *whether or not* the trains are stopping in those countries. • Every client has a right to discharge his or her lawyer at any time for any reason or no reason at all, *irrespective of the fact whether or not* any money is owed. Every client has a right to discharge his or her lawyer at any time for any reason or no reason at all, *regardless of whether* any money is owed. • Kundalini is present in the body of all persons *irrespective of the fact whether* they are ordinary persons or highly spiritual persons. Kundalini is present in the body of all persons *whether* they are ordinary persons or highly spiritual persons.

46. is dependent on (upon) *depends on; hinges on.*

• You shouldn't *be dependent upon* anyone else for your happiness. You shouldn't *depend on* anyone else for your happiness. •

The position of the object of a phrasal verb *is dependent on* whether or not the phrasal verb is separable or inseparable. The position of the object of a phrasal verb *depends on* whether or not the phrasal verb is separable or inseparable. • The Morton Grove Days Committee's annual budget ($40,000 to $50,000) *is dependent upon* the size of the July 4th parade and fireworks, and the costs related to the festival activities. The Morton Grove Days Committee's annual budget ($40,000 to $50,000) *depends on* the size of the July 4th parade and fireworks, and the costs related to the festival activities.

47. is -ing delete.

• What the kids *are wanting* is to be loved. What the kids *want* is to be loved. • We have gained a much better understanding of what providers *are seeking* from our networks, and we *are looking* forward to presenting our plan. We have gained a much better understanding of what providers *seek* from our networks, and we *look* forward to presenting our plan. • Today, millions of Americans with disabilities *are engaging* in productive, gratifying endeavors. Today, millions of Americans with disabilities *engage* in productive, gratifying endeavors. • Some *are speculating* that Apple's new device is a digital music product for its iTunes software, while others think Apple may unveil a PDA, a Web pad — or even a set top box. Some *speculate* that Apple's new device is a digital music product for its iTunes software, while others think Apple may unveil a PDA, a Web pad — or even a set top box.

48. is what delete.

• While consistency is the mainstay of our program, diversity and change *are what* keep it exciting. While consistency is the mainstay of our program, diversity and change keep it exciting.
• The person-machine interface *is what* must be retained if security is not to become a purely mechanical effort. The person-machine interface must be retained if security is not to become a purely mechanical effort. • Another major group *is what* Ogbu calls autonomous minorities. Another major group Ogbu calls autonomous minorities. • This type of learning process *is what* is suggested for this preliminary activity. This type of learning process is suggested for this preliminary activity. • The daily behavior of good citizens *is what* holds society together. The daily behavior of good citizens holds society together.

49. (a; the) key...in (of; to) *(a) key to*.

• Market segmentation is a *key aspect to* strategic planning at the corporate and business levels. Market segmentation is a *key to* strategic planning at the corporate and business levels. • In contrast, individualism was *the key ingredient to* the rise of Greece. In contrast, individualism was *key to* the rise of Greece.
• Our continued commitment to quality is a *key component of* our success. Our continued commitment to quality is a *key to* our success.

50. less than (enthusiastic) *dis-; il-; im-; in-; ir-; mis-; non-; un-*.

• You can refinance with us even if your credit is *less than perfect*. You can refinance with us even if your credit is *imperfect*. • This book reveals the sometimes *less-than-elegant* design of DOS by walking through the source code. This book reveals the sometimes *inelegant* design of DOS by walking through the source code. • The lack of consistent definition and the paucity of carefully designed drug studies of PMS have led to *less than satisfactory* treatment. The lack of consistent definition and the paucity of carefully designed drug studies of PMS have led to *unsatisfactory* treatment.

51. (a; the)... level (of) delete.

• Each organization must assess its *level of* willingness to take risks. Each organization must assess its willingness to take risks. • When a relationship reaches a certain *level of* intensity, the church should have some way of recognizing that commitment. When a relationship reaches a certain intensity, the church should have some way of recognizing that commitment. • Random access implies that any piece of information can be read with *an* equal *level of* difficulty and delay. Random access implies that any piece of information can be read with equal difficulty and delay.

52. like... for example (for instance) *as; for example (for instance); like; such as*.

• The drug is good for ailments *like insomnia for example*. The drug is good for ailments *like insomnia*. • It is not that fascinating, as it uses a standard approach to computing in XSLT, but its advantage is that it works also with XSLT processors (*like, for instance,* James Clark's XT) that do not have the "node-set" extension function implemented. It is not that fascinating, as it uses a standard approach to computing in XSLT, but its advantage is that it works also with XSLT processors (*for instance,* James Clark's XT) that do not have the "node-set" extension function implemented. • The atoms of ferroelastic materials are arranged in a way that points in one direction in space, *for example like* a series of stacked chevrons. The atoms of ferroelastic materials are arranged in a way that points in one direction in space, *like* a series of stacked chevrons.

53. -(al)ly speaking *-(al)ly;* delete.

• All four of their parents would be the same, *genetically speaking.* All four of their parents would be *genetically* the same. • Although there may be small differences between the jobs, they are, *relatively speaking*, inconsequential. Although there may be small differences between the jobs, they are *relatively* inconsequential.
• *Personally speaking,* I belonged to the Howdy Doody generation. I belonged to the Howdy Doody generation.

54. make . . . (a; the) . . . (about; of; to) delete.

• Why *make that admission to* them? Why *admit that to* them? • We *made an agreement* that she would keep the stereo for me. We *agreed* that she would keep the stereo for me. • The company's management may not see any reason for *making a shift* from their current approach. The company's management may not see any reason for *shifting* from their current approach. • *Make an estimate of* what the person might find if the process were revamped to operate as well as is conceivable. *Estimate* what the person might find if the process were revamped to operate as well as is conceivable. • The nurse was *making an adjustment to* his IV solution. The nurse was *adjusting* his IV solution.

55. (a; the) -ment of *-ing*.

• *The assignment of* retirement assets to a money manager may entail a lengthy process of evaluation by the corporate client. *Assigning* retirement assets to a money manager may entail a lengthy process of evaluation by the corporate client. • Meetings do not contribute to *the attainment of* individual objectives. Meetings do not contribute to *attaining* individual objectives. • *The treatment of* these items as expenses results in lower rents and more available apartments. *Treating* these items as expenses results in lower rents and more available apartments.

56. more preferable *preferable*.

• We have never said any one group is *more preferable* to another. We have never said any one group is *preferable* to another. • Reorganization of the health care industry still remains one of the alternatives being considered because structural and procedural changes are often *more preferable* than basic, radical changes in the philosophy behind such a system. Reorganization of the health care industry still remains one of the alternatives being considered because structural and procedural changes are often *preferable* to basic, radical changes in the philosophy behind such a system.

57. mutual... and (between... and; both; each other; one another; two) *and (between... and; both; each other; one another; two).*

• I think all three news directors in town have a *mutual respect for one another.* I think all three news directors in town have a *respect for one another.* • Understanding exists when *both parties involved in the communication mutually agree* not only on the information but also on the meaning of the information. Understanding exists when *both parties involved in the communication agree* not only on the information but also on the meaning of the information. • You can live with many differences of opinion and personal style if you and your partner have *mutual respect for each other's abilities.* You can live with many differences of opinion and personal style if you and your partner have *respect for each other's abilities.* • It's time to begin the healing process, time to bridge the gap of miscommunication, and time to cultivate an atmosphere of *mutual respect between law enforcement and our communities.* It's time to begin the healing process, time to bridge the gap of miscommunication, and time to cultivate an atmosphere of *respect between law enforcement and our communities.*

58. notwithstanding the fact that *although; but; even though; still; though; yet.*

• Of what relevance to usage (*notwithstanding the fact that* the topic is interesting) is an entry on eponyms? Of what relevance

to usage (*though* the topic is interesting) is an entry on eponyms?
• Unless a confession is given freely and rationally, it will be inadmissible *notwithstanding the fact that* it is reliable. Unless a confession is given freely and rationally, it will be inadmissible *even though* it is reliable.

59. numerous in number *numerous.*

• These lines are lower voltage than the high power lines, but they are much more *numerous in number.* These lines are lower voltage than the high power lines, but they are much more *numerous.* • The lesions may be few or *numerous in number,* reddish or brownish in color, with a surface that is usually smooth and shiny, but may sometimes be dry and rough with scales. The lesions may be few or *numerous,* reddish or brownish in color, with a surface that is usually smooth and shiny, but may sometimes be dry and rough with scales.

60. obtain (a; the) ... (for; of; to) delete.

• Using the first number less than 3.257 and the first number greater than 3.257, it is possible to *obtain an approximation for* log 3.257 by using linear interpolation. Using the first number less than 3.257 and the first number greater than 3.257, it is possible to *approximate* log 3.257 by using linear interpolation. • In order to *obtain an understanding of* the antiquity of Clan MacKay, we must first look at Ireland's history, which according to many historians, makes the history of all other countries look infantile by comparison. In order to *understand* the antiquity of Clan

MacKay, we must first look at Ireland's history, which according to many historians, makes the history of all other countries look infantile by comparison.

61. obviate the necessity (need) for (of; to) *obviate (-ing)*.

• Of course, an awareness of this uncertainty doesn't *obviate the need to make* decisions based on your best guess about what the future holds. Of course, an awareness of this uncertainty doesn't *obviate making* decisions based on your best guess about what the future holds. • NAS 4 and its support for Enterprise Java Beans *obviates the need for* the solution proposed in this chapter. NAS 4 and its support for Enterprise Java Beans *obviates* the solution proposed in this chapter. • The Active Directory support *obviates the need to register* a component locally for use on a remote server. The Active Directory support *obviates registering* a component locally for use on a remote server.

62. (a; the)...of *-ing*.

• For most American families, this means *an analysis of* the costs of operating and financing their automobiles. For most American families, this means *analyzing* the costs of operating and financing their automobiles. • Even more important is *a knowledge of* the costs of consumption in terms of the alternative consumption opportunities that are given up because of the particular choices made. Even more important is *knowing* the costs of consumption in terms of the alternative consumption opportunities that are given up because of the particular choices made.

63. of... dimensions (magnitude; proportions; size) delete.

• It was a success *of monumental dimensions.* It was a *monumental* success. • The mess surrounding our president is a tragedy *of substantial proportions.* The mess surrounding our president is a *substantial* tragedy. • Manny Ramirez hit a homerun *of historic proportions.* Manny Ramirez hit a *historic* homerun. • If He did not return when He said He would, we have a dilemma *of huge proportions.* If He did not return when He said He would, we have a *huge* dilemma. • A storm *of monstrous proportions* developed in the Atlantic that year and several ships were caught in its fury. A *monstrous* storm developed in the Atlantic that year and several ships were caught in its fury. • For those of you who don't know, World War II was an event *of immense magnitude* in world history. For those of you who don't know, World War II was an *immense* event in world history.

64. of (a; the) ...nature delete.

• This type of analysis is of recent origin and is primarily *of a conceptual rather than analytical nature.* This type of analysis is of recent origin and is primarily *conceptual rather than analytical.* • It was found that the material in his shoe was *of an explosive nature.* It was found that the material in his shoe was *explosive.* • First-level management deals with *day-to-day operations of a repetitive nature.* First-level management deals with *repetitive day-to-day operations.*

65. on a (the)... basis *-(al)ly;* delete.

• The exercises must be done for 20 to 25 minutes *on a continuous basis.* The exercises must be done *continuously* for 20 to 25 minutes. • Every exchange has a clearinghouse that transfers funds from losers to winners *on a daily basis.* Every exchange has a clearinghouse that transfers funds *daily* from losers to winners. • Our sole interest in the report is to be sure that each application is evaluated *on a fair basis.* Our sole interest in the report is to be sure that each application is evaluated *fairly.* • It has been estimated that, *on a worldwide basis,* banks and credit card companies lose $3 million annually. It has been estimated that, *worldwide,* banks and credit card companies lose $3 million annually. • Questions as complex as the ones contained in this collection cannot be graded *on a right or wrong basis.* Questions as complex as the ones contained in this collection cannot be graded *right or wrong.* • We will continue to add features to the site and update information *on a frequent basis.* We will continue to add features to the site and update information *frequently.*

66. (something; somewhere) on the order (of) *about; around; close to; more or less; near; nearly; or so; roughly; some;* delete.

• Typically, the ratio of injury to mortality is *something on the order of* three or four to one. Typically, the ratio of injury to mortality is *some* three or four to one. • I counted *something on the order of* 50 interruptions for applause. I counted 50 *or so* interruptions for applause. • For software whose development time is *on the order of* two years, there are two possible arrangements. For software whose development time is *around* two years, there are two possible arrangements.

67. on the part of *among; by; for; from; in; of; -'s;* delete.

• Though deliberate discrimination *on the part of* the Japanese is often charged, it isn't necessary to prove a discriminatory intent. Though deliberate discrimination *by* the Japanese is often charged, it isn't necessary to prove a discriminatory intent. • The effective teaching of language arts requires a commitment to excellence *on the part of* the classroom teacher. The effective teaching of language arts requires a commitment to excellence *from* the classroom teacher. • His apt observations point out the need for greater *awareness on the part of the public* of the architecture that surrounds them. His apt observations point out the need for greater *public awareness* of the architecture that surrounds them. • How has *the practice of these concepts on your part* affected the way you live, and how has *the practice of these concepts on the parts of other people* affected the way you perceive the world? How has *your practice of these concepts* affected the way you live, and how has *other people's practice of these concepts* affected the way you perceive the world?

68. over the course (duration; length) of *during; for; in; over; throughout; when; while; with.*

• *Over the duration of* the project, we expect there will be some disruption due to noise, dirt, and dust. *During* the project, we expect there will be some disruption due to noise, dirt, and dust. • *Over the course of* her extraordinary career, much has been made of Madonna's multifaceted attributes and abilities. *Throughout* her extraordinary career, much has been made of

Madonna's multifaceted attributes and abilities. • *Over the course of* the next two hours, a further half dozen of these tremendously bright meteors were seen. *Over* the next two hours, a further half dozen of these tremendously bright meteors were seen.

69. past (previous; prior) experience *experience.*

• A shortage of workers for jobs requiring little skill is forcing some employers to hire people without considering their references, *past experience,* or education. A shortage of workers for jobs requiring little skill is forcing some employers to hire people without considering their references, *experience,* or education. • I have no *prior experience* working with children. I have no *experience* working with children. • AvaQuest's principals have extensive *previous experience* working with clients in both the government and commercial sectors. AvaQuest's principals have extensive *experience* working with clients in both the government and commercial sectors.

70. perform (a; the) ... of delete.

• He *performed an extensive analysis of* the financing patterns of U.S. corporations. He *extensively analyzed* the financing patterns of U.S. corporations. • Then *perform a comparison of* the two disks. Then *compare* the two disks. • If an order is executed, the database *performs the clearing of* the trade within an escrow account. If an order is executed, the database *clears* the trade within an escrow account. • In the first part of the book, Gray offers strategies for empowering staff, boards, volunteers, and clients to *perform an evaluation of* their organization. In the first part of the book, Gray offers strategies for empowering staff, boards, volunteers, and clients to *evaluate* their organization. • For example, you could *perform a study of* the EMF/leukemia link with animals. For example, you could *study* the EMF/leukemia link with animals.

71. **place (put) (a)... (in; into; on; under; upon)** delete.

• In determining the relative quality of municipal securities, many investors *place great reliance on* the rating provided by the two major rating agencies. In determining the relative quality of municipal securities, many investors *greatly rely on* the rating provided by the two major rating agencies. • The Act only covers the actual cost of cleaning up pollution damage, and does not *put a limit on* compensation claims from third parties. The Act only covers the actual cost of cleaning up pollution damage, and does not *limit* compensation claims from third parties. • The result can be the gradual accumulation of policies and practices that, like a bad diet, overload the organs and *place burdens on* the members struggling to keep it alive. The result can be the gradual accumulation of policies and practices that, like a bad diet, overload the organs and *burden* the members struggling to keep it alive.

72. **place (put) a priority on (upon)** *appreciate; cherish; esteem; favor; highly regard; prefer; prize; rate highly; respect; treasure; value.*

• We need to *place a priority on* education at all levels. We need to *prize* education at all levels. • Look for developers who *put a priority on* producing the best product for you and your customers. Look for developers who *value* producing the best product for you and your customers. • We urge newsroom managers to *place a priority on* diversity as hiring opportunities present themselves. We urge newsroom managers to *favor* diversity as hiring opportunities present themselves. • We will always *place a priority on* simplifying the learning process and motivating educators. We will always *highly regard* simplifying the learning process and motivating educators.

73. predict ahead of time (beforehand; in advance) *predict.*

• I'm not privy to the secret of how to *predict ahead of time* who will succeed. I'm not privy to the secret of how to *predict* who will succeed. • Since the impedance change may vary with frequency, there is no way of *predicting in advance* how the modulation percentage will vary across the spectrum. Since the impedance change may vary with frequency, there is no way of *predicting* how the modulation percentage will vary across the spectrum. • For some applications, you cannot *predict in advance* how many connection pools you will need. For some applications, you cannot *predict* how many connection pools you will need.

74. (then) proceed (to) *later; next; then;* delete

• The team *proceeded to* develop the recently generated ideas into a concrete curriculum. The team developed the recently generated ideas into a concrete curriculum. • He *proceeded to* declare his undying love for me. He *then* declared his undying love for me. • The two *proceeded to* examine the intriguing sample through dissecting microscopes, when suddenly Professor Armstrong noticed a tiny green speck among the larger duckweeds. The two *next* examined the intriguing sample through dissecting microscopes, when suddenly Professor Armstrong noticed a tiny green speck among the larger duckweeds. • Bobby Bonds entered the game during the fourth inning to replace starter Billy Williams, then *proceeded to* smack a two run homer during his first at-bat in the fifth inning off California's Bill Singer. Bobby Bonds entered the game during the fourth inning to replace starter Billy Williams, then smacked a two run homer during his first at-bat in the fifth inning off California's Bill Singer.

75. (a; the)...process delete.

• It's been *a* gradual *process*. It's been gradual. • *The* assessment *process* involves rigorously examining the methods used. Assessment involves rigorously examining the methods used. • Getting into the honesty business, in short, can be *an* expensive and arduous *process*. Getting into the honesty business, in short, can be expensive and arduous. • Doctors should not dismiss complaints of incontinence as an inevitable part of *the* aging *process*. Doctors should not dismiss complaints of incontinence as an inevitable part of aging. • It is *an* extremely frustrating *process* to define a new exception in a low-level class and then have to edit and recompile all the classes that use this class. It is extremely frustrating to define a new exception in a low-level class and then have to edit and recompile all the classes that use this class. • You'll find that making your own ice cream is *an enjoyable and rewarding process,* although it takes practice, and vanilla is the perfect place to start. You'll find that making your own ice cream is enjoyable and rewarding, although it takes practice, and vanilla is the perfect place to start.

76. put an end (a halt; a stop) to *cease; close; complete; conclude; end; finish; halt; settle; stop.*

• In the last century, liberals fought to *put an end to* the cruel traffic in human flesh known as slavery. In the last century, liberals fought to *end* the cruel traffic in human flesh known as slavery. • Before things get out of hand again this year, let's try to *put a halt to* it now. Before things get out of hand again this year, let's try to *halt* it now. • I want you to *put a stop to* all of this nonsense. I want you to *stop* all of this nonsense.

77. (a) question mark *enigma; mystery; puzzle; question; uncertain; unknown; unsure.*

• For scientists trying to forecast how the world will react to the burgeoning burden of greenhouse gases, clouds pose a vexing *question mark*. For scientists trying to forecast how the world will react to the burgeoning burden of greenhouse gases, clouds pose a vexing *question*. • "It's up in the air," Poole said when asked if he would attempt to play this week. "It's *a question mark*." "It's up in the air," Poole said when asked if he would attempt to play this week. "It's *uncertain*."

78. (the) reason (why)...is because *because; reason is (that).*

• *The reason* the business failed *was because* it was undercapitalized. The business failed *because* it was undercapitalized. • Another *reason why* the example fails as a good strategic goal *is because* it violates the rule of accountability. Another *reason* the example fails as a good strategic goal *is* it violates the rule of accountability. • The *reason is because* most players have little knowledge about the game and even less about money management. The *reason is that* most players have little knowledge about the game and even less about money management. • Part of the *reason why is because* of the Internet's inability to handle the transfer of the enormous amount of data requested of it daily. Part of the *reason is* the Internet's inability to handle the transfer of the enormous amount of data requested of it daily.

79. regardless of who (whom) *despite who (whom); no matter who (whom); whoever (whomever).*

• *Regardless of who* we may be, we all have the right to economic opportunity. *Whoever* we may be, we all have the right to economic opportunity. • *Regardless of whom* these books are meant for, they should be designed and developed to look and feel more accessible. *Despite whom* these books are meant for, they should be designed and developed to look and feel more accessible. • The country will survive, *regardless of who* is in White House. The country will survive, *no matter who* is in White House.

80. relatively...compared (contrasted) to (with) *compared (contrasted) to (with); -(i)er than (less than; more than).*

• Shrinkage remains *relatively low compared to* mass retailing standards. Shrinkage remains *low compared to* mass retailing standards.
• They tend to have a relatively high loss and PDL, and are *relatively expensive compared to* mechanical switches. They tend to have a relatively high loss and PDL, and are *more expensive than* mechanical switches. • In fact, Mathers and Bank still stay in close contact with other cast members, and their lives are *relatively stable compared with* those of other former child stars. In fact, Mathers and Bank still stay in close contact with other cast members, and their lives are *stable compared with* those of other former child stars. • Although the UK is *relatively small when compared with* the United States, its landscape and people are varied and dramatic; what it lacks in physical size it makes up for in culture, history, etc. Although the UK is *smaller than* the United States, its landscape and people are varied and dramatic; what it lacks in physical size it makes up for in culture, history, etc.

81. reminisce about the past *reminisce.*

• Families *reminisce about the past* in different ways and the parent's reminiscing style influences the child's reminiscing style. Families *reminisce* in different ways and the parent's reminiscing style influences the child's reminiscing style. • NostalgiaStreet.com's mission is to provide a friendly place where people can *reminisce about the past* while enjoying today and preparing for tomorrow. NostalgiaStreet.com's mission is to provide a friendly place where people can *reminisce* while enjoying today and preparing for tomorrow.

82. report back *report*.

• The Insurance Division will *report back* to the high court within 30 days on whether to rehabilitate them in some ways or declare them insolvent. The Insurance Division will *report* to the high court within 30 days on whether to rehabilitate them in some ways or declare them insolvent. • Most Cobol programs will validate the end user's input and *report back* any invalid input to the end user. Most Cobol programs will validate the end user's input and *report* any invalid input to the end user. • The AMA will *report back* to the House of Delegates on the status of this public-private entity as appropriate. The AMA will *report* to the House of Delegates on the status of this public-private entity as appropriate.

83. separate and distinct *distinct; separate*.

• Each of us has four *separate and distinct* vocabularies: a written, a spoken, a heard, and a visual vocabulary. Each of us has four *distinct* vocabularies: a written, a spoken, a heard, and a visual vocabulary. • The creature, though *separate and distinct*, and having its own jurisdiction, cannot arise and consume its creator. The creature, though *separate*, and having its own jurisdiction, cannot arise and consume its creator.

84. (a; the) -sion (-tion) of (that; to) *-ing*.

• *Determination of* consumer's needs requires greater attention. *Determining* consumer's needs requires greater attention. •

Their subordinates are nonmanagement workers — the group on which management depends for *the execution of* their plans. Their subordinates are nonmanagement workers — the group on which management depends for *executing* their plans. • Self-improvement and career planning both begin with *an identification of* your skills. Self-improvement and career planning both begin with *identifying* your skills. • I would suggest that, given the importance of building confidence in these tradesmen-turned-entrepreneurs to the proposal, *inclusion of* more background on them would be a good idea. I would suggest that, given the importance of building confidence in these tradesmen-turned-entrepreneurs to the proposal, *including* more background on them would be a good idea.

85. (a; the)…situation delete.

• We are in *a crisis situation*. We are in *a crisis*. • If he doesn't do something, it could be *an embarrassing situation* for him. If he doesn't do something, it could be *embarrassing* for him. • It's really *a pathetic situation*. It's really *pathetic*. • If there is an *emergency situation,* then that person can exit as well. If there is an *emergency,* then that person can exit as well. • It's nice to be *in a situation where you are recognized* for the work you're doing. It's nice to be *recognized* for the work you're doing. • The *air conditioning situation* is currently under repair. The *air conditioner* is currently under repair. • The network approach *is a win-win situation for* all involved. The network approach *benefits* all involved.

86. such as…for example (for instance) *as; for example (for instance); like; such as.*

• One of the book's main themes is the "fact" that women were responsible for all the important contributions to the advancement of civilization (*such as* the development of agriculture, *for instance*), often despite the arrogance and stupidity of men. One of the book's main themes is the "fact" that women were responsible for all the important contributions to the advancement of civilization (*such as* the development of agriculture), often despite the arrogance and stupidity of men. • If a substance is not on our chart (*such as* vanadium, *for example*), it's not yet considered essential by the National Academy of Sciences. If a substance is not on our chart (vanadium, *for example*), it's not yet considered essential by the National Academy of Sciences. • They also don't support other advanced elements of FrontPage Web sites, *such as* input forms, *for example.* They also don't support other advanced elements of FrontPage Web sites, *such as* input forms.

87. the extent to which *how; how far; how much; how often.*

• *The extent to which* these facilitating and reconciling capabilities are needed, and how they are developed and structured, depends on the company's involvement in exporting or foreign marketing. *How much* these facilitating and reconciling capabilities are needed, and how they are developed and structured, depends on the company's involvement in exporting or foreign marketing. • Eastern cannot predict *the extent to which* its oper-

the manner (means; mechanism; method; procedure; process) by (in) which 45

ations and financial results will continue to be affected by the negative public perception generated by the investigations. Eastern cannot predict *how* its operations and financial results will continue to be affected by the negative public perception generated by the investigations.

88. the manner (means; mechanism; method; procedure; process) by (in) which *how.*

• I'm not going to discuss *the methods by which* we achieved that. I'm not going to discuss *how* we achieved that. • The philosophical methodology specifies *the procedure by which* concepts will be used to construct a theory. The philosophical methodology specifies *how* concepts will be used to construct a theory. • It does less well in explaining *the process by which* a particular firm decides to implement a price change. It does less well in explaining *how* a particular firm decides to implement a price change. • Virtually all of them have been critical of *the manner in which* the administration dealt with the situation. Virtually all of them have been critical of *how* the administration dealt with the situation.

89. the ... of -*'s.*

• I needed *the help of my mother* to care for my child. I needed *my mother's help* to care for my child. • *The task of the analyst* is to find the coefficients a and b in Equation 2-2. *The analyst's task* is to find the coefficients a and b in Equation 2-2. • The failure to recognize expenses of this type can affect *the profitability of a product.* The failure to recognize expenses of this type can affect *a product's profitability.*

90. **the process of** delete.

• *The process of* selecting the proper school for your child can be hugely exciting. Selecting the proper school for your child can be hugely exciting. • For many people, trading in their current car plays an important role in *the process of* purchasing a new car. For many people, trading in their current car plays an important role in purchasing a new car.

91. **there is…(that; who)** *is;* delete.

• *There are* fifteen people in the group. Fifteen people *are* in the group. • *There are* millions of people *who* feel the way you do. Millions of people feel the way you do. • For every discovery that scientists make about Egyptian antiquity, *there are* hundreds *that* remain unsolved. For every discovery that scientists make about Egyptian antiquity, hundreds remain unsolved. • *There's* a healthy percentage of public investors *who* are interested and participate in the market throughout their lives. A healthy percentage of public investors are interested and participate in the market throughout their lives.

92. **the thing is** delete.

• *The thing* is we know sexual orientation is discovered prior to adolescence. We know sexual orientation is discovered prior to adolescence. • *The thing is* I work two jobs, and when I get home I want to relax. I work two jobs, and when I get home I want to relax. • But *the thing is,* there's always someone who knows where they are. But, there's always someone who knows where they are.

93. to a great (large) degree (extent) *almost all; chiefly; commonly; generally; greatly; in general; largely; mainly; most; mostly; most often; much; nearly all; normally; overall; typically; usually; well.*

• *To a large extent,* the success of any business venture depends on planning. The success of any business venture *chiefly* depends on planning. • I see the source of hope in a movement that's building around the country, *to a large extent* among young people in colleges and even high schools. I see the source of hope in a movement that's building around the country, *largely* among young people in colleges and even high schools. • Because the state will pay for the bulk of building and running the school, it will naturally be involved in the project *to a large degree.* Because the state will pay for the bulk of building and running the school, it will naturally be *much* involved in the project. • In Malaysia, imports are controlled *to a great degree* by a handful of European commission houses. In Malaysia, imports are *mostly* controlled by a handful of European commission houses.

94. to make (a; the)... (about; of; on; with) *to; to -(al)ly.*

• I need *to make a correction about* something I said yesterday. I need *to correct* something I said yesterday. • I wanted *to make a comment* on his appearance. I wanted *to comment* on his appearance. • We will give the audience a chance *to make inquiries* about this. We will give the audience a chance *to inquire* about this. • I will do everything possible *to make a thorough evaluation of* your application. I will do everything possible *to thoroughly evaluate* your application. • I am eager *to make a deal*. I am eager *to deal*.

95. until such point (time) as *until*.

• Instead of a 50-percent pay raise, they should have a 50-percent pay cut *until such time as* they rule with honesty, integrity, and compassion. Instead of a 50-percent pay raise, they should have a 50-percent pay cut *until* they rule with honesty, integrity, and compassion. • Discussions will continue *until such point as* I have something to show on paper. Discussions will continue *until* I have something to show on paper.

96. (a; the) vital…in (of; to) *vital in (to)*.

• We have been very pleased with their performance and have found them to be *a vital part of* our operation. We have been very pleased with their performance and have found them to be *vital to* our operation. • Reforming the intelligence community is *a vital element in* waging an effective war on terror. Reforming the intelligence community is *vital to* waging an effective war on terror.

97. what is... (is that) *-(al)ly;* delete.

• *What* we need *is* a way to go directly to the partition block. We need a way to go directly to the partition block. • *What* we have described *is* a typical, hierarchical, central-processor-based, online architecture. We have described a typical, hierarchical, central-processor-based, online architecture. • *What is* not so clear or commonly accepted is the scope and nature of these obligations. Not so clear or commonly accepted is the scope and nature of these obligations. • If a broadband LED signal is sent through a filter, *what* comes out *is* only the portion of the LED spectrum that is passed by the filter. If a broadband LED signal is sent through a filter, only the portion of the LED spectrum that is passed by the filter comes out. • *What* create static electricity *are* different potentials. Different potentials create static electricity.

98. when it comes to *about; as for; as to; concerning; for; in; of; on; over; regarding; respecting; to; toward; when; with*; delete.

• She's very shy *when it comes to* performing in front of an audience. She's very shy *about* performing in front of an audience. • Employers, employees, and society are often in conflict *when it comes to* dealing with five key issues facing them today in the workplace. Employers, employees, and society are often in conflict *over* dealing with five key issues facing them today in the workplace. • Being terrible with names is not an option *when it comes to* naming your book. Being terrible with names is not an option *when* naming your book.

99. while at the same time (concurrently; simultaneously) *as; at the same time; concurrently; simultaneously; while.*

• Our aim is to help professional and semi-professional freelance writers promote their work to thousands of publications worldwide, *while simultaneously* providing editors with a valuable resource for written material. Our aim is to help professional and semi-professional freelance writers promote their work to thousands of publications worldwide, *while* providing editors with a valuable resource for written material. • Women's colleges are offering women innovative programs, *while at the same time* they are opening doors for minorities. Women's colleges are offering women innovative programs, *while* they are opening doors for minorities. • *While* getting signatures, volunteers were *simultaneously* assessing the degree of support for my candidacy. *While* getting signatures, volunteers were assessing the degree of support for my candidacy. • A message can be sent to the driver vectoring her to a repair center, *while concurrently* a message is sent to the repair center alerting it to the car's arrival. A message can be sent to the driver vectoring her to a repair center, *as* a message is sent to the repair center alerting it to the car's arrival.

100. with regard to *about; as for; as to; concerning; for; in; of; on; over; regarding; respecting; to; toward; with;* delete.

• The evidence is mixed *with regard to* the existence of an optimal capital structure. The evidence is mixed *on* the existence of an optimal capital structure. • *With regard to* the first rationalization, how can a manager know how far is too far? *As to* the first rationalization, how can a manager know how far is too far?

101. with the purpose of -ing *for (-ing); so as to; to.*

• The writer wrote the article *with the purpose of teaching* American businesspeople about Japanese gifts. The writer wrote the article *to teach* American businesspeople about Japanese gifts. • The first common schools were opened *with the purpose of preparing* the population for citizenship. The first common schools were opened *so as to prepare* the population for citizenship. • The same technology was used in a civilian application *with the purpose of saving* lives. The same technology was used in a civilian application *for saving* lives.

The Vocabula Review

If you've enjoyed this book, you may want to subscribe to *The Vocabula Review* (www.vocabula.com), an online journal about the English language. Twelve monthly issues of *The Vocabula Review* cost only $12.00.

Mail this page (or a photocopy of it) with your check or money order — made payable to Vocabula — to:

> The Vocabula Review
> 5A Holbrook Court
> Rockport, MA 01966

Name: _____

Email address: _____
(please print clearly)

Once we've received your payment, we will email you a password so that you can read *The Vocabula Review*'s pages.

The Vocabula Review
www.vocabula.com

Vocabula Books

Please send me the following books:

Title	Price	Quantity
101 Wordy Phrases	$7.95	_____
101 Foolish Phrases	$7.95	_____
101 Elegant Paragraphs	$7.95	_____
Vocabula Bound Quarterly	$50.00 (a year)	_____

Add $3.00 for postage, and mail this page (or a photocopy of it) with your check or money order — made payable to Vocabula — to:

> Vocabula Books
> 5A Holbrook Court
> Rockport, MA 01966

Name: _____

Address: _____

_____

Email address: _____
(please print clearly)

Vocabula Books
an imprint of
Vocabula Communications Company